CITY MACHINES

JACKHAMMERS

Connor Dayton

PowerKiDS
press
New York

Published in 2012 by The Rosen Publishing Group, Inc.
29 East 21st Street, New York, NY 10010

First Edition

Editor: Jennifer Way
Book Design: Ashley Drago

Photo Credits: Cover, p. 5 © www.iStockphoto.com/Mike Clarke; p. 6 © www.iStockphoto.com/ Werner Stoffberg; pp. 9, 24 (top left) © www.iStockphoto.com/Jim Jurica; p. 10 Ethan Miller/ Getty Images; pp. 13, 16–17, 22, 24 (bottom right) Shutterstock.com; pp. 14–15, 24 (top right) © www.iStockphoto.com/Alexandr Dvorak; p. 18 © www.iStockphoto.com/Don Bayley; pp. 21, 24 (bottom left) U.S. Department of Defense/Science Faction/Getty Images.

Library of Congress Cataloging-in-Publication Data

Dayton, Connor.
Jackhammers / By Connor Dayton. — First Edition.
    pages cm. — (City Machines)
Includes index.
ISBN 978-1-4488-4957-4 (library binding) — ISBN 978-1-4488-5064-8 (pbk.) —
ISBN 978-1-4488-5065-5 (6-pack)
1. Jackhammers—Juvenile literature. I. Title.
TJ1305.D39 2012
621.9'52—dc22
                                        2010048484

Manufactured in the United States of America

CPSIA Compliance Information: Batch #WS11PK: For Further Information contact Rosen Publishing, New York, New York at 1-800-237-9932

CONTENTS

Jackhammers are used in **construction** work.

Jackhammers break up rocks and concrete.

Jackhammers are used to fix roads and sidewalks.

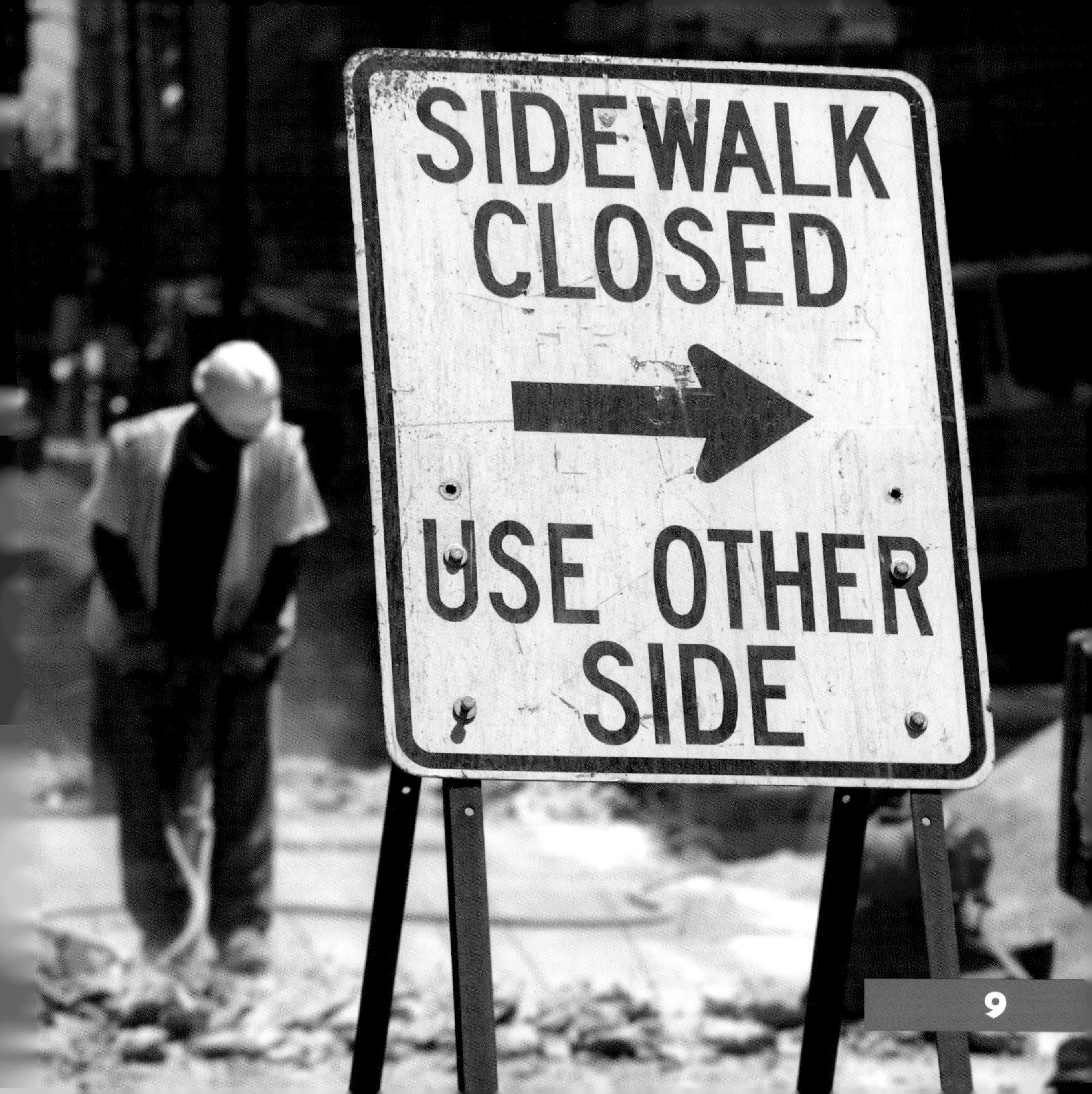
SIDEWALK
CLOSED
USE OTHER
SIDE

A motor pushes air through a hose. The air goes into the jackhammer.

Air moves the hammer up and down. The hammer moves very fast!

13

The **drill bit** is at the jackhammer's tip. Drill bits come in many shapes.

Not all jackhammers are handheld. **Excavators** use big jackhammers.

Jackhammers on excavators do big jobs.

Jackhammers are loud! People must wear **earplugs** when using jackhammers.

People wear hard hats when using jackhammers. These keep workers safe.

WORDS TO KNOW

INDEX

WEB SITES

Due to the changing nature of Internet links, PowerKids Press has developed an online list of Web sites related to the subject of this book. This site is updated regularly. Please use this link to access the list:
www.powerkidslinks.com/city/jackham/